# METAMORPHOSIS

# METAMORPHOSIS
## A Life Journey

Poetry by
Pat J. Schulz

ENHEART PUBLISHING

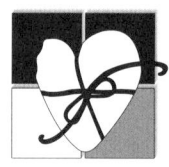

ENHEART PUBLISHING
P. O. Box 560576
Charlotte, NC 28256–0576

Copyright © 1996 by Pat J. Schulz. All rights reserved, including the right of reproduction in whole or in part in any form.

Printed in the United States of America

Library of Congress Catalog Card Number
96-90745

ISBN:    0-9654899-0-6

*Cover art and logo design by Rick Lyon*

This chronolog of poetry is dedicated
in memory of

I%%RENE J%%ULIA M%%ARGARET F%%ERGUSON

whose passing birthed a void.
In its place comes these works.

# ACKNOWLEDGMENTS

*To all the friends, family, and strangers I've come to know. Thank you for sharing your gifts with me. Each of you have truly been an inspiration.*

*Particular gratitude goes to:*
*E. Lynn Harris, Steve Knickerbocker and Robin Tran for planting vision seeds.*

*A group of special individuals who lovingly edited while in its truest form:*
*Dr. Clifford A. Jones, Michelle Jones, Adriene Mervin, Dana V.C. Mervin, K.D. Mervin and Joyce B. Sewell.*

*Ed Bohannon, Michelle Myers, and Rick Lyon without you the vision would not be reality.*

*Janice Standifer and Shay Whitmire - you are gems.*

*Annette Norwood—for immeasurable support.*

*Most of all my greatest thanks is given to The Creator, whose divine spirit inspired me to produce these works and to share my gift with you.*

# A NOTE FROM THE AUTHOR

*Metamorphosis*

*This one word characterizes the life journey of all living things. It represents change in our lives as we grow, mature and come into the fullness of who we are and who we are meant to be. Change may not always be welcome, but it is necessary and imminent if we are to grow. I have used the medium of poetry to transcribe emotions that accompany change in one's life.*

*Growth is not an easy thing—we have growing pains. But, when you come into your knowing, each experience of pain, joy, love, and disillusionment can be placed in its proper perspective. What you gain from it all is uniquely yours. What you gain is uniquely you.*

*As you join this experience with me keep this thought in mind—*

*Welcome your metamorphosis.*

# CONTENTS

### PHASE ONE
A Petal is Formed      1
—*The maturing process*

### PHASE TWO
In the Spring She Blossoms      9
—*A flower in love*

### PHASE THREE
The Summer Scorches      33
—*A burn hurts*

### PHASE FOUR
Then Comes the Fall      43
—*A melancholy mood as a result of lost love*

### PHASE FIVE
The Winter Rejuvenates      57
—*A time to be restored*

### PHASE SIX
God Is the Creator of All Life's Seasons      65
—*The Alpha and Omega*

# METAMORPHOSIS

PHASE ONE

A Petal
Is Formed

*Where have you come from?*
*And where are you going?*
*Why did our paths cross?*
*Just wherein is our knowing?*

*The questions do rise.*
*The answers will fall.*
*Truth gently doth lay*
*Upon the death of us all.*

*Whether we choose to listen*
*To obey, to adhere*
*Is the decision we embrace*
*To partake or to fear.*

*The answers to all mysteries*
*Lie within our reach.*
*If only we take the time*
*To learn and to teach.*

*Surely morning will come*
*And love brings light to day.*
*But, only after an eve of the moon*
*Does a ray appear to lead the right of way.*

## Metamorphosis

*Those little nasty*
*Four letter words*

*You know,*
*The ones*
*We live with intimately*
*Those that become*
*Akin to our very core*

*Yet, we camouflage our familiarity*
*Beneath the screen of conformity*

*Control becomes the key . . .*
*The challenge of the day . . .*

*We dare not share that*
*We have not mastered*
*Control over four letter words*

*Love,*
    *Loss,*
        *Fear,*
            *Tear*

## A Petal Is Formed

*It is our tears*
*Hiding the fear*
*Of every loss*
*Of love*

*If only I knew*
*You suffered too*

*Then our familiarities*
*Would be in conformance*

*We could shed our coat*
*Of intimate camouflage*
*And those four letter words*
*Would no longer be nasty.*

## Metamorphosis

*Because he is different*
*We pretend he does not exist*
*Society names him an outcast*
*Yet, his spirit remains in our midst*

*He feels like you and I*
*His blood flows and flesh is real*
*Though because of our ignorance*
*His identity he must conceal*

*This man without a face*
*Whose kindness generates fear*
*What a pity he is*
*To those who lurk and leer*

*They know not the man*
*Nor the knowledge he holds*
*It is society's loss*
*For his riches are sealed untold*

*Be careful how you treat a stranger*
*For within a friend may lie*
*Beyond the vacancies of those*
*Unidentified, distant eyes.*

## A Petal Is Formed

*Friends*
*They come and go*

*A true one*
*Is hard to know*

*Some*
*Can be a*
*Blessing in disguise*

*Others*
*Deceive you*
*In front of your very eyes*

*Be careful*
*How you choose*

*For a foe*
*Has nothing to lose*

*But,*
*A true friend*
*Is like a treasure*

*Its value*
*Is ageless*

*And beauty*
*Lasts forever*

*How does one become known?*

*Learn to know Yourself*

*Accept Yourself*

*Then, you are known unto Yourself*

*Only then can others know You*

*For the truth that You are.*

PHASE TWO

# In the Spring She Blossoms

*Each time you hold me near*

*Another petal opens*

*And I continue to grow*

*Into a brighter, fuller*

*More beautiful*

*May Flower*

## Metamorphosis

*Your eyes undressed me*
*Very slowly, intimately, very sensuously.*

*They touched me*
*In a most gentle way.*

*Your lips spoke silently*
*The most assuring words.*

*Whispering delightful sighs*
*Softly to my ear.*

*And in our imaginations*
*We made precious love*
*In the most innocent way.*

*Only a capsule of time*
*Spent with you*
*Unleashes desires*
*That lay patiently dormant*

*Just enough*
*To remember*
*What love once was*
*What love could be*
*Recalling the enactment*

*In only a capsule of time*
*Captivated by you*
*I relive not having love*
*Otherwise known as torment*

## Metamorphosis

*A warm fall breeze*
*Calmly blew you into my life.*
*Blanketing my soul*
*With a mist of love's delight.*
*Spreading your wings*
*You silently invited me in.*
*Having highest anticipation*
*This fresh beginning*
*Would not come to an abrupt end.*
*A sprinkle of heaven's golden dust*
*Gave me insight as the breeze began to gust.*
*And as you revealed yourself to me,*
*The breeze spread into a raging sea.*
*Delivering a unique love*
*That could only be sent by such highness above.*
*As the breeze eased and serenely fell,*
*It left me to cherish a beautiful,*
*Golden Angel.*

*From the moment we met*
*I was intrigued*
*It was your starlit eyes*
*That planted the seed*

*The confidence in your voice*
*The gleam in your smile*
*All of these*
*Made me want to stay with you a while*

*For I knew there was much more*
*Than the tenderness*
*Of your kiss*

*More than the gentleness*
*Of your touch*
*More than this*
*Yes, much more ever to adore*

*For all of these drew me nigh*
*To the closeness of you*
*And*
*Yet*
*The mystery remains*
*Fresh, vibrant and anew*

## Metamorphosis

*Never imagined friends*
*Could become lovers*

*Never thought a friend*
*Could be a lover*
*To a friend's lover*

*But, friends and lovers*
*I have found*
*Can be one in the same*

*Never considered the shame*
*To be a lover*
*Of a friend's lover*

*But now, I realize*
*I loved you, my friend*
*Long before I became your lover*

*Tenderness you are*
 *Tender on my heart*


   *Brightness in my life*
   *Lightly to my soul*


       *Lovingness you bring*
       *Giving of yourself*


           *Tender I become*
           *Just beneath your heart*

## Metamorphosis

*Had a dream*
*Of you and I*
*So peaceful it was*
*A tranquil high*

*We were lying*
*On the shore*
*Making love*
*To the rhythmic flow*
*Of the tide*

*And time was no more*
*It only stood still*
*Cherishing the precious moments*
*Of two lovers in a dream*

*Your tender touch*
*Sends me into the new heaven*
*I've often dreamt of so much.*

*Where I could lie naked*
*In a field of deep evergreen grass*
*With dandelions about.*
*And the bright yellow sun shines down,*
*But, the peaceful wind camouflages its heat.*

*Beside me, there you lie;*
*So close I felt I were melting*
*Into you.*

*Being held in your strong yet, gentle arms.*
*Near to your smooth golden skin,*
*I smile placidly;*
*And all you see*
*Is my warm*
*But,*
*Slight smile.*

# Metamorphosis

*A touch of soft baby's skin*
*Frictioning blazing flames within.*

*A tender lift across a calm ocean wave*
*Sauntering within a deep dark cave.*

*A natural simultaneous movement*
*Gliding along the summer wind's passive contentment.*

*A most desirable satisfying touch of plush velveteen*
*Kissing you sets the suppressed flicker free.*

*'Want to touch your face*
*Against my breast*
*Ever so tenderly . . .*

*'Want you to stroke my body*
*With the patience of a clockmaker*
*In perfect time and rhythm . . .*

*More than anything*
*'Want to touch your*
*Heart and soul once again . . .*

*Like the first moment you wanted me*
*So desperately,*
*You cried in need of me . . .*

## Metamorphosis

*Inspiration*
*That's what you are*

*Moving me to desire*
*Moving me to require*

*More and more of you*

*Inspiration*
*That's what you are*

*Moving me toward mountains*
*Moving me, releasing fountains*

*Of joy and more and more of me*

*Inspiration*
*You certainly are*

*Moving more than you could ever imagine*

*Moving a woman*
*Takes more than imagination*

*It takes inspiration*

*Whispers in the dark*
*Melodies of grandeur*
*Rise & fall*
*Like the tunes of a morning lark*

*And I rise & fall*
*With each octave*
*Responding to your every move*
*Your sound, your every call*

*Each moment is one to rejoice*
*Overcome by your passion*
*I am swept away by*
*The midnight whispers of your voice*

## Metamorphosis

*Sometimes my love is so deep,*
*So strong, so mellow*
*It sings a song*
*For you to hear*

*But, I wonder if you're*
*Catching the tunes as they*
*Flow by your ear*

*I can feel the words*
*As they are silently*
*Captured in the air around us*

*But, I can't help wonder*
*If you're touching the notes*
*As I do*

*For if you are not*
*If you cannot*
*See the words*
*Or the tune*

*Just lie your head*
*Upon my breast*
*This love will beat*
*Before you*

*As a drummer*
*Who plays*
*Virtuously obsessed*

*Falling*
> *would not be the correct term*
> *for these emotions*
> *that colorfully burn*

>> *. . . when I am with you*

*I am Rising*
> *to an all time high*
> *far beyond the clouds*
> *into the ozone*

>> *. . . when you draw nigh*

*Inflated*
> *by your touch*
> *I rise to meet you*
> *at the golden arches*

>> *. . . the cornerstone of love*

*No, I am not Falling*
> *in love with you*
> *I rise like a dove*

>> *. . . I Rise*

## Metamorphosis

*I know the exact moment*
*When I fell in love with you*

*The air blew brisk*
*Yet, I was warm*

*The sky was dark*
*Yet, I saw light*

*We had just met*
*But, I had known you a lifetime*

*I know the exact moment*
*When I fell in love with you*

*The heavens fell upon me*
*A million twinkling stars*

*Yet, it only took one*
*To make a dream*
*Come true*

*Beauty Lies In*

*The*

*Warmth Of The*

*Sun's Rays*

*And*

*The Brightness*

*Of*

*Your Smile*

## Metamorphosis

*Only in Paradise*
*Do the stars*
*Sparkle a rainbow of colors*
*Before our eyes*

*Only in Paradise*
*Can the waters*
*Calm our busy*
*Souls and minds*

*And only in Paradise*
*Could I lie with you*
*Under the moonlit sky*
*Without one care*

*Only knowing . . .*
*Time quickly passes*
*With two passionate lovers*
*In the nature of . . .*

*Jamaican Paradise*

*Central Park
In the dark
Strangers stroll
Lives unfold*

*Under rain's subtle mist
I am wettened by a kiss*

*Sharing dreams
Alive, yet broken
As it seems*

*Dancing by dawn
Closely in your arms
I slowly arise
To first meet your eyes*

*By fate
I've found a special friend*

*Too late
At the Grand Plaza it ends*

## Metamorphosis

*If you go away*
*Just leave me your hand*

*A small part of you*
*That brought so much pleasure*

*The artist at work*
*Molding and shaping*
*His sculptress of love*

*Here I lie formed by*
*The sweet touch of your inspiration*

*Lying almost lifeless*
*Because it is your touch*
*That makes me come alive*

*If you must go*
*Do leave your hand*
*By my side*

*If I go away,*
*I will not be gone to stay,*
*I'll leave you with special moments*
*Of loving times we've spent.*
*A smile, a laugh, a tear . . .*
*A love, strong and dear . . .*
*A lasting kiss*
*Tenderly missed . . .*
*And a soft gentle touch*
*You'll yearn for so very much.*
*A favorite song will remind you of me.*
*Lonely, only for the moment you may be.*
*But, my dear, I will not be far away.*
*Look into your heart.*
*I'm there to stay.*

PHASE THREE

# The Summer Scorches

## The Summer Scorches

*Sometimes I idealize*
*About the times we once knew*

*Desperately optimizing*
*I imagine us making mellow love*
*On a bed*
*Of sweet yellow roses*

*As the heat swelters*
*The flowers begin to wilt*

*And nothing remains*
*But, heart throbbing thorns*

## Metamorphosis

*When the rain comes...*

*Memories fall down on me*
*It's like getting caught*
*In an Indian summer shower.*

*At first slow drops*
*And then,*
*Before you know it*
*You're covered*
*Head to toe*

*So goes the fallen memories*
*First one*
*Then another*
*And before you know it*
*You're all caught up*
*In heart drenching memories.*

*When the rain comes...*

*Realizing love is sometimes hard to do.*
*It's often difficult to be sure someone is loving you.*
*And when you love that someone,*
*Proving your love may be easier said than done.*

*Many times it takes*
*A bit of heartache*
*To bring you to the light of love,*
*That is so often taken for granted and shunned.*

*Once I heard that the process of this realization*
*Can put you through a change*
*That sometimes hits a spot left unguarded.*
*And leaves a little pain.*

*I remember staring into your hurt eyes.*
*And, there was nothing more to realize.*

*I saw love.*

## Metamorphosis

*You took the love I had*
*Spit it in your hand*
*Wiped it on a filthy wall*
*Said "I'm sorry,"*
*And ran.*

*You fled to never-never land*
*Leaving me behind*
*To face the world alone*
*So yourself you could find.*

*But, only if you knew*
*That part of you is in me*
*And you'll never be whole*
*Until you see*
*I hold part of your identity.*

*With love, I am reborn*
*I sing with the birds*
*Float on the clouds*
*Feel as soft as a baby*
*Nothing is as radiant as I*
*When I am in love*

*But, when you take it away*
*I cannot sing*
*Too heavy to float*
*All feeling is gone*
*When you take love away*
*I cease to exist*

## Metamorphosis

*Magical moments do come to pass*
*Although they may not always last*

*Such moments are destined, lovely and true*
*As destiny willed me to love you*

*We both knew in time*
*Our souls would beat in rhythm and rhyme*

*Together we have reached the mountain top*
*The climb was so high*
*I thought I could not stop*

*Just as I reached the peak*
*I felt the magic of love began to leak*

*Drip,   drop*
            *s*
              *l*
                *o*
                  *w*
                    *l*
                      *y*

_____The Summer Scorches

*Draining from the depths of my soul*

*The wound opens deeper*
*I'm no longer able to control*

*Drip,    drop*
*             the rhythm*
*                           s*
*                            l*
*                             o*
*                               w*
*                                s*

*I am beginning to fold*

*Stripped naked*
*Mind, body and soul*

*The magic ends.*

*But, why does it take your soul*
*And leave broken hearts?* ⚘

## Metamorphosis

*We must all come to know,*

    *come to terms,*

        *come to accept,*

            *come to live with our pain as*

*part of the intimacy of knowing ourselves. We must embrace the pain, mourn the pain, rock the pain, until it is soothed to where we learn to carry it around without having the thorns dart into us when least expected. When we learn to do this, the thorns vanish one by one. Until one day you see your pain metamorphose into a gentle flower.*

*With one eye viewed as too delicate to touch.*

*But, with a closer eye you will see a remarkable strength of resiliency held by each petal.*

*Each petal joined together creates a marvelous thing of beauty.*

### This is MY PAIN.

PHASE FOUR

# Then Comes the Fall

*Your love made me blossom*
*Like honeysuckle on the vine*
*Your love produced nectar of the gods*
*And with careless pleasure*
*You partook of the wine*

*Your selfish taking*
*Sapped the suppleness*
*Out of our love*

*After the blossom dried*
*Under the blistering summer's heat*
*What else could I do*
*But, give way to*
                THE

           FALL ✤

## Metamorphosis

*Your Motto:*
*Keep Life Simple*

*Yet, you are so complicated.*

*One moment your love overflows.*

*The next you are as distant*

*As a diffusing galaxy.*

*How I long to touch*

*Those twinkling stars within.*

*To find what makes you*

*So unique as you are.*

*In my longing*

*My desire turns*

*To frustration*

*And my love*

*Begins to*

*Fade.*

*When I required excitement*
*In my life*
*I summoned you.*

*Yes, I admit*
*My eyes beckoned you come near.*

*Your touch*
*Was more than I could bear.*

*Yet,*
*One touch of your lips*
*One touch of your electrifying fingertip*
*On my thigh was not enough*

*Let the excitement begin . . .*

*And now I feel so sad to ask,*

*Where has it gone?*
*Where did it end?*
*Will I ever touch your tenderness again?* ❖

## Metamorphosis

*i made love to you*
  *— you called it having fun*

*i undressed my inhibitions*
  *— you call it strip poker*

*i fell in love*
  *— you thought it was a game* ❦

*Devil in a blue suit*
*Lookin' all good*
*Yeah, he's kinda' cute*

*Smooth talkin' business man*
*Confidence exudes him*
*And I'm his biggest fan*

*He sways me his way*
*One request is all it takes*
*And I've fallen into his game*

*Trapped beneath the*
*Glass ceiling of love*
*There's only so far you can go*

*When you're dealing with*
*An elusive devil*
*In a blue suit* ❧

# Metamorphosis

*If a mountain of words could erase a memory*
*You would see a mountain*

*If a flood of tears could wash away a moment*
*You would see a fountain*

*If I held the power of the gods*
*Time would have stood still*
*In the day we met*

*Of these powers*
*I have none*
*But, of one I do know*
*There is, but one*

*Love has the power to*
*Bring forth the beauty*
*In us all*

*Love is the power that lifts us up*
*When we fall*

*Love alone can break the chain*
*That binds us apart from one another*

*In the moment I thought I lost you*
*True love came shining through*

*So bright I could not bear*
*Not to have you there*

*If I could only take this love*
*And manifest it in your heart*
*What power that would be*

## Then Comes the Fall

*If love can create a rainbow*
*Perhaps, it can make one for us too*
*Whatever it would take*
*That is what I would do*

*If you ever believed there was*
*Something special about us*
*Something special for us*
*Believe that love can create a miracle*

*A miracle can change a heart*
*It can lift and bless*
*Only love can create a happiness*

*These words come from my heart*
*Though not enough to make a mountain*
*Nor enough to wash a stream*
*But I hope just enough to mend a dream*

*That you and I once shared*
*Not too long ago*
*A beautiful life*
*I really don't want to let go*

*They say strong love*
*Is stronger than strong walls*
*If we can hold on to one another's hand*
*The power of love won't allow us to fall*
                *Not ever . . . again*

## Metamorphosis

*He said he cared*
*But, he never did*
*The little things that show it.*

*He said he cared*
*But, I never saw him*
*Until . . .*

*He said he cared*
*Right before he had*
*To go home.*

*He said he cared*
*But, he left me for another.*

*He said he cared*
*And someday I would make*
*Someone very happy.*

> *You said you cared*
> *You wanted to stay.*
> *I wouldn't let you.*
> *You brought me flowers.*
> *They faded.*
> *You wanted to make me happy*
> *Someday . . . like today.*

*But, I didn't want you*
*I was too distracted over all the others that*
*Cared !?* ✿

*Who was it that lied*
*Saying my Prince*
*Would someday come?*

*Who was it that lied*
*Saying I would grow up*
*To be a heart breaker?*

*I've looked forward to*
*Meeting my prince*
*Sought him behind the eyes*
*Of each and every suitor*

*But, he was not there*

*I looked forward to discovering*
*The power I was to have*
*That would protect my heart*

*I looked forward to discovering*
*The power I was to have*
*That could control another's*

*But, I tell you someone lied to me*

*Princes don't exist*
*And the only heart that gets broken is mine*

## Metamorphosis

*Today I thought of you . . .*
*And could no longer hear*
*The sound of your voice.*

*I tried to remember . . .*
*Could see your lips move*
*There was no sound.*

*Lost in time . . .*
*A distant place*
*There is no evidence.*
*There is no trace . . .*

*Only an inaudible memory.* ❀

*Someone touched my heart*

*In a special way*

*And left it*

*Throbbing in the dark*

PHASE FIVE

# The Winter Rejuvenates

## The Winter Rejuvenates

*The winter is a time for renewal*
*A time to rest*
*Put away old things*
*And restore for the new*

*I met you in the winter*
*A time when I was love fatigued*
*Worn from battle*
*Daring to love again*

*You brought me sunshine*
*On a snow cloudy day*
*It was the warmest winter*
*I've ever known*

*Resurrected from my past*
*Your eternal embrace*
*Brought me new life*

*And I shall always remember*
*That winter day*
*How you awakened me*
*From my heartbroken slumber*

*And told my heart*
*It is spring*

## Metamorphosis

*Finally I am getting myself together*
*No longer am I up under the weather*
*Used to drown myself in tears*
*Floods of foolish hopes and fears*

*Maybe my rainbow isn't as bright*
*But, at least my direction is right*
*I'm headed in the path of reality*
*And dreams no longer overshadow me*

*Yes, I am finally finding my way to the light*
*And it is going to be hard*
*Not having you in my life*

*Because of you . . .*

*I am glad life's uncertainties*
*Have led me to a different path*

*In a world full of constant change*
*We never know what we will find along the journey*

*But, I am certain that you and I*
*Were meant to be at some point in time*

*Because of you . . .*

*I am glad the time is now*
*And yes,*

*If only for now*

## Metamorphosis

*Life is strange with its twists and quirks*
*We search for love*
*To bring all its joys and perks*

*We never expect love to fail*
*Only to take wings*
*Those delicate wings to sail*

*Still we search for strength*
*To accept whatever may come*

*Strength to welcome new love*
*And strength to let go*
*When those precious wings of love*

*Fade into the mist . . .*

## The Winter Rejuvenates

*I dreamt of water.*
*Huge waves of powerful water.*
*Approaching unexpectedly,*
*The unstoppable movement stunned me.*
*And I stood there in awe of its beauty.*

*Waiting in anticipation.*
*Knowing I could not fight it, nor escape it.*
*I waited for this massive piece of nature*
*To sweep me up and take me on its journey.*

*In that moment, we became one.*
*I flowed with its beauty and power.*
*In that moment, I became all powerful.*

*Knowing,*
*I no longer had to run or overcome.*
*I had the power of acceptance.*

PHASE SIX

# God Is the Creator of All Life's Seasons

_____God Is the Creator of All Life's Seasons

*Little Words Mean So Much*

<u>L</u> *iving*

    <u>I</u> *n*

        <u>F</u> *aith*

            <u>E</u> *ternally*

<u>*God gives LIFE*</u>

# Metamorphosis

*Have you ever sent a wail out*
*To the Lord?*
*Such a loud cry that you*
*Could feel the sound of waves*
*Moving throughout the universe*

*God heard your wail*
*And sent His angels*
*To reply*

*They came to lift your burden*
*Angels came 'cause you were hurting*

*I know you sent a wailing*
*I can see the stain marked in your eyes*

*I looked into them and saw a reflection of mine*

*If I can't meet you half way
I'll just see you on the other side
I'll greet you at the gate
I'm sure you won't mind.*

*It'll be easier
When we shed our earthly skin
We'll have new names
You can call me then.*

*Call me by my new name
See me as your sister in the Lord
Love is everlasting
Don't you wanna get on board?*

*I hope to see you there
The land of milk and honey
They say the streets are paved with gold
And every day is sunny.*

*But, I often stop and wonder
If we couldn't meet on earth
Will there be a place at the gate?
You know
By then
It may be too late.*

## Metamorphosis

*Only by faith*
*Can we run this race*

*Only by grace*
*Can we lead the race*

*Only by seeking God's face*
*And His glory within*

*Can we triumph life's experiences*
*And discover the victorious win*

*Although the winds may blow*
    *Its sails to and 'fro*

*And the uncertainties of nature*
    *May cause the ship*
    *To detour from the*
    *Way it should go*

*The All Merciful guides*
    *The ship ashore*
    *With grace and ease*

*All look to marvel at its strength*
    *Oh mighty ship*
    *Thou art*

*They wonder at its splendor*
    *And ask how did she*
    *Get such a part*

*If they only knew through*
    *Stormy gale and*
    *Lightning's mist*
    *She came*

*The landing is too short lived*
    *To carry her fame*

*True glory is found*
    *In the journey*

# Metamorphosis

*The Spirit Within
A Part of Me*

*GOD's*

*Blessed Trinity*

*God Is the Creator of All Life's Seasons*

*King Jesus knows my needs,*
*Supply them that He will.*
*The true desires of my heart*
*He promised to fulfill.*

*But, I must walk along His path.*
*Let His hand be my guide.*
*Ask protection by His staff;*
*Knowing He is always by my side.*

*I will trust in the Lord*
*For all power does He hold.*
*And I see Him working daily,*
*Blessing as my life unfolds.*

*Trusting only in Him*
*To quench my every need.*
*And yes,*
*Giving something in return;*
*Always praises given*
*In human kindness and in deed.*

## Metamorphosis

*On bended knee
We give praises to Thee
Gratitude is shared
By two whose love
God has paired*

*His spirit sent a shining light
To guide me to the love
For my life*

*Yes, I did pray
For the one for me
Send him, Lord now
Send him, ever so quickly*

*He did not answer
Right away
Years had past
My blessing was in delay*

*Yet, God had laid it
On my heart
That I shall be whole
With true love to impart*

*But, I had some
Lessons to learn
Mysteries unfolded
Some blessings you must earn*

## God Is the Creator of All Life's Seasons

*Someone told me*
*God is preparing the two of you*
*Be patient and discerning*
*This is something you must do*

*To hold the wisdom*
*And an open mind*
*Was my prayer to keep*
*Until you I'd find*

*And tonight I hold*
*On to your hand*
*While I bow to*
*Thank our Lord*
*For answering prayer*

*A gift of love*
*He promised to send*
*Years of searching*
*Have come to an end*

*It was His spirit*
*That told me so*
*I heard an angel's voice*
*Saying with you I should go*

*This voice brought me peace*
*I knew it must be fate*
*To lead me on a journey*
*With my lifetime love*
*My spiritual soulmate.*

# Metamorphosis

*This day marks the beginning*
*Of the rest of our lives*
*You as my husband*
*And I as your bride*

*To have and to hold*
*To love and adore*
*Our love is forever*
*Until time is no more*

*For God has annointed*
*The bond of us two*
*He pours down His blessings*
*When we say I do*

*No greater happiness we've known*
*Before Christ entered our lives*
*His love has made all the difference*
*Bonding two souls - yours and mine*

*Totally devoted*
*I surrender all my love to you*
*This day we will cherish*
*A day when dreams come true*

*Of All God's Wonders*

*The Most Miraculous Are*

*Life and Love*

*and*

*The Giving of These*

# ABOUT THE AUTHOR

Pat J. Schulz is a resident of Charlotte, North Carolina, where she is active in community service. She serves on the Women's Commission Domestic Violence Advisory Board and is a leader in the American Business Women's Association. She is employed as an Accounting Manager in the insurance industry. Her leadership has been acknowledged with a host of awards and positions. She is a graduate of the University of North Carolina at Greensboro, where she received a B.S. degree in Business Administration.

Pat began creative writing at an early age of twelve, shortly after the passing of her mother. This talent has been nurtured over the years, and used by the author as a personal outlet. She is a member of the North Carolina's Writer's Network and the International Society of Poets. *Metamorphosis: A Life Journey* is Schulz' first published work. You will find her work published in *Memories of Tomorrow*, an anthology by The National Library of Poetry. Additionally, her poetry is to be featured on "The Sound of Poetry"—audio series.

## ORDER FORM

Name: _____
Address: _____
City: _____
State: _____
Zip: _____

**Sales Tax:**
Please add 6% for books shipped within North Carolina

**Shipping:**
# of books _____ at $11.95 per book
$2.95 shipping first book, $.75 for each additional

**Payment:** Enheart Publishing
( ) check    ( ) money order    ( ) cashier check

**Mail Payment to:** ENHEART PUBLISHING
                    POST OFFICE BOX 560576
                    CHARLOTTE, NC 28256-0576

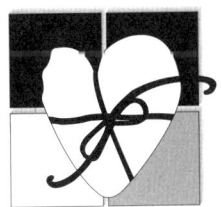